Novels for Students, Volume 37

Project Editor: Sara Constantakis Rights Acquisition and Management: Margaret Chamberlain-Gaston, Jackie Jones Composition: Evi Abou-El-Seoud

Manufacturing: Rhonda Dover

Imaging: John Watkins

Product Design: Pamela A. E. Galbreath, Jennifer Wahi Content Conversion: Katrina Coach Product Manager: Meggin Condino

© 2011 Gale, Cengage Learning

ALL RIGHTS RESERVED. No part of this work covered by the copyright herein may be reproduced, transmitted, stored, or used in any form or by any means graphic, electronic, or mechanical, including but not limited to photocopying, recording, scanning, digitizing, taping, Web distribution, information networks, or information storage and retrieval systems, except as permitted under Section 107 or 108 of the 1976 United States Copyright Act, without the prior written permission of the publisher.

Since this page cannot legibly accommodate all copyright notices, the acknowledgments constitute an extension of the copyright notice.

For product information and technology assistance, contact us at **Gale Customer Support, 1-800-877-4253.**

For permission to use material from this text or product, submit all requests online at www.cengage.com/permissions.

Further permissions questions can be emailed to **permissionrequest@cengage.com** While every effort has been made to ensure the reliability of the information presented in this publication, Gale, a part of Cengage Learning, does not guarantee the accuracy of the data contained herein. Gale accepts no payment for listing; and inclusion in the publication of any organization, agency, institution, publication, service, or individual does not imply endorsement of the editors or publisher. Errors brought to the attention of the publisher and verified to the satisfaction of the publisher will be corrected in future editions.

Gale
27500 Drake Rd.
Farmington Hills, MI, 48331-3535

ISBN-13: 978-1-4144-6700-9

ISBN-10: 1-4144-6700-1
ISSN 1094-3552

This title is also available as an e-book.
ISBN-13: 978-1-4144-7366-6
ISBN-10: 1-4144-7366-4
Contact your Gale, a part of Cengage Learning sales representative for ordering information.

Printed in Mexico
1 2 3 4 5 6 7 15 14 13 12 11

The Age of Innocence (Film)

Edith Wharton 1993

INTRODUCTION

Critics and audiences were surprised in 1993 to find that Martin Scorsese, the director best known for such gritty, contemporary urban dramas as *Mean Streets, Taxi Driver*, and *Good-fellas*, had chosen to direct a film adaptation of Edith Wharton's 1920 tragicomedy of manners, *The Age of Innocence*. Wharton's novel deals with repressed feelings among society's upper ranks in New York in the 1870s, while Scorsese's most common themes involved machismo and violence—for instance, 1991's *Cape Fear*, featuring frequent Scorsese collaborator Robert De Niro as a psychotic murderer and rapist. The resulting film ended up on many critics' ten-best lists at the end of the year, and it was nominated for several Academy Awards.

Scorsese, who had been given the book by coscreenwriter Jay Cocks, found an emotional connection with Wharton's close and careful examination of social rituals, and his expert control of cameras and actors helped bring Wharton's writing alive for many viewers who otherwise might not have read her novel. The basic story, about a man who is engaged to marry one woman but finds himself falling in love with another, is familiar to any age, but Scorsese uses it, as Wharton did, to comment on the ways in which one can be imprisoned within a society of almost endless wealth. In the hands of stars Michelle Pfeiffer, Daniel Day-Lewis, and Winona Ryder, along with a strong supporting cast, *The Age of Innocence* brings out what the Gilded Age and the modern world have in common.

PLOT SUMMARY

The Situation

The Age of Innocence opens with a title card that says "New York City, the 1870s." After establishing that the setting is at an opera (Charles Gounod's *Faust*, which premiered in Paris in 1859 and was new to New York at the time), the camera focuses on a boutonniere on a man's tuxedo coat, pulling back to reveal that it belongs to Newland Archer. Archer is seated in his club's box at the opera house, among other men in similar clothes. Sillerton Jackson, later revealed to be a gossip, notices Madame Olenska in the Welland box while he is scanning the audience with his opera glasses, and he makes a suggestive comment.

Archer goes over to the Welland box and talks to his fiancée, May Welland. He wants to announce their engagement, but she mentions her mother's opposition. May introduces Archer to her cousin, Madame Ellen Olenska, but she already knows Archer from childhood.

After the opera ends, all of the people leave for the annual opera ball at the Beaufort mansion. Scorsese's camera takes in the formalities of the ball. Archer hurries to the Beaufort house to quickly announce his engagement, to direct gossip away from Madame Olenska. Archer, the narrator explains, privately questioned conformity, though publicly he upheld family and tradition. He counted on May to be his moral guide.

Later, May and Archer go to Mrs. Manson Mingott to announce their engagement. In addition to being May's grandmother, she is one of the most famous and well-connected women in New York society. Mrs. Mingott is pleased that the Archer family will be joined with the Welland family, since they are two of the most prominent families in the city. As they leave her house, the camera draws back to show her five-story, block-wide mansion, surrounded by the undeveloped flat land in all directions that was New York north of Central Park at that time.

Sillerton Jackson dines with Archer, his mother, and his sister, who are too shy to venture into society themselves. They gossip about the Beauforts, but then the talk changes to Madame Olenska. Archer defends her divorce when the others make disparaging remarks about it. Later, when the men are alone smoking cigars, they discuss how the family secretary took Madame Olenska away from the womanizing Count Olenski. Jackson is scandalized, but Archer still defends her.

Mrs. Mingott sends out invitations to all of the society families in New York to come to a dinner to meet the Countess Olenska. The dinner is a failure, however, when everyone declines her invitation. The Welland family is disgraced. Archer goes to the van der Luydens, one of the most powerful society families, to explain that Larry Lefferts has caused society to turn against the Wellands. When

Lefferts's wife suspects him of bad behavior, Archer explains, Larry usually starts rumors about someone else, to deflect attention. Mr. van der Luyden, seeing the slight as an injustice, offers to invite Countess Olenska to their own party for a visiting duke the following week, to present her to society.

Madame Olenska arrives late for the dinner, flouting social rules. She is uncomfortable until Archer comes to sit with her. Before he leaves, Madame Olenska invites Archer to her home the following day.

Archer arrives early and looks over her modern and primitive art pieces. As they talk, she invites him to sit near her and offers him a cigarette, and they both smoke. Discussing her difficulty fitting into society, she wells up with tears, and Archer puts his hand on hers. She withdraws slowly.

That night, passing his usual florist, Archer sends flowers to May, as he always does, and then sends another bouquet to Madame Olenska.

The Affair

Casually, Archer tells May that he sent flowers to Madame Olenska. May is surprised, since her cousin mentioned flowers from several people but never mentioned receiving any from him.

Archer is assigned by his superior at his law firm, Mr. Letterblair, to consult with Countess Olenska about her divorce. He is apprehensive, but he is told to try to steer her away from pursuing a divorce from Count Olenski because the scandal with the Count's secretary might be dragged up.

Archer visits Madame Olenska and suggests that she could be hurt by the Count's accusations in a divorce, even if the accusations are unfounded. She notices that he uses the word "if," uncertain about the truth about the Count's claims, about her innocence. Since the Count is in Europe and she is in America, Archer tells her to leave the situation alone. She agrees to do as he advises.

FILM TECHNIQUE

- As is customary for a Martin Scorsese picture, the camera is very seldom still in *The Age of Innocence*. Even in scenes where the actors are standing or sitting still, the camera is usually moving around them, examining their faces, objects in the room, or objects outside the window. In enclosed areas, where the camera could not be mounted to a stable track, Scorsese makes use of the Steadicam. The Steadicam is an invention introduced in 1976 to help camera operators stabilize the film's image and provide smooth motion. This device allows camera operators to move around the actors with hand-held cameras without capturing the natural unevenness of human motion that would result in bumps and bounces on the film.

- Scorsese also makes use of the 360-degree tracking effect, in which the camera, mounted on a track on the floor, circles around its subjects. One conspicuous scene that uses this type of shot is the lunch at the Mingott estate, after Archer has refrained from approaching Madame Olenska as she stands by the ocean. As polite conversation carries on, the camera moves around the table, taking in each speaker while Archer suppresses his anguish.

- Several times in this film, Scorsese ends a scene using the irising effect that was popular with films of the silent era, particularly in the films of early director D. W. Griffith. With this technique, the camera's lens can be seen closing, creating a circle of darkness that contracts around the scene, usually closing entirely to black the screen out. When Archer and Madame Olenska meet in the balcony during the play, for instance, about forty-eight minutes into the film, Scorsese uses the irising effect to close out the talk of the others in their box just as Archer is closing out the chatter of everyone but her. The reverse effect is used to show how intensely Mrs. Mingott's attention is focused on May's wedding ring before the circle opens up, showing the rest of the room.

- Because this film involves a world of almost unimaginable wealth, Scorsese uses a rich color palette, especially in the opening scenes. The opera house is lined with a deep, velvety red and trimmed with gold, and those two colors carry over to the following scene, in the Beaufort mansion. Most of the indoor scenes have dark backgrounds and include some form of dark red and gold, colors associated with royalty.

- Scorsese ends a few scenes with a color fade. Though most film audiences are familiar with the "fade to black," this film fills the screen with bright colors, to show the emotions that are arising out of the dark backgrounds. When Madame Olenska opens the bouquet of yellow roses from Archer, for instance, the camera shows a look of satisfaction on her face before the screen fades to yellow. When the camera shows Madame Olenska while the narrator discusses how her family suffered a social "eradication," she turns to the camera and the scene fades to red.

- In presenting a society in which emotions are not openly discussed, the film resorts to close-up shots of objects, faces, and gestures. The close-up focuses the viewer's attention on details without commenting on them. Scorsese uses many close-ups in this film, from the gloves and food given to party guests to the tentative touch of hands that gives unexpressed hope to Archer and Ellen Olenska. The frequent, fluid movement from standard shots to close-ups is a sign of the film's storytelling artistry.

At the theater, watching a melodrama about two lovers parting, Archer is stricken with emotion. Regina Beaufort calls him up to the box where Countess Olenska sits off to the side, by herself. She mentions the yellow roses he sent, wondering if the man in the play might send yellow roses to his lover. She also mentions that May is away for her annual trip to Florida.

The next day, Archer tries to send Countess Olenska more yellow roses, but they are not available. She does not answer his letters, and he feels rejected, but after a few days she sends him a letter saying she is staying at a house upstate. Archer goes there and finds her alone. For a moment, as they talk, he imagines her coming and putting her arms around him. He sees Julius Beaufort approaching the house and is jealous. Everyone assumes that Beaufort, a womanizer, is involved with Madame Olenska, though his appearance at the upstate house turns out to be only for a real estate matter.

Archer goes to St. Augustine, Florida, to be with May. As she talks, he tunes her voice out, but then he implores her to marry him soon. She says that she has felt since the became engaged that he is interested in someone else. Archer assures her that he has no other lovers. "There is no one between us," he tells her.

Archer goes to Mrs. Mingott to ask her to support an early marriage. Mrs. Mingott tells him about the possibility that Madame Olenska might reunite with her husband, joking that Archer should have married her instead of May. On the way to the door, he takes Madame Olenska aside and asks with urgency when they can see each other.

At her house that night, he eventually admits his feelings for Madame Olenska. She angrily accuses him for being the one to tell her to forget about divorce. He points out that he is still free and that she can be, too, and they kiss. When she breaks away from him, she explains how he has helped her fit into society, describing her fear that an affair with him will take away the goodness in him. While she talks, Archer bends down and kisses her foot.

The Marriage

A telegram from May announces to Countess Olenska that her parents have agreed to move the wedding up. The Countess does not attend the wedding. On their honeymoon in Europe, Archer notices that May is increasingly traditional, making decisions about their lives based on social standing. He looks back on his relationship with Countess Olenska as "the madness" and an "experiment."

Back in New York, they visit Mrs. Mingott. She sends for Madame Olenska, who has been staying with her, only to find that she has left the house. Mrs. Mingott sends Archer to find her. Although it has been a year and a half since they last saw each other, the sight of her, with the sunlit water behind her, stirs up the old feelings. He tells himself that he will go to her only if she turns around before a passing boat reaches the lighthouse; when the boat goes by, he returns to the house and says that he could not find her.

The Wellands are invited to visit the Blenkers, the family that Madame Olenska is staying with. Knowing where she lives, Archer goes to the home to find her, but she has gone to Boston. He lies to the young Blenker girl to find out where she will be in Boston and goes there to find her. When they meet, Archer finds out that Count Olenski's secretary has been sent to America to offer her money to return to the Count.

Archer and Madame Olenska have lunch together and are very open about their feelings for each other. Madame Olenska takes hold of Archer's hand and then leaves.

In a montage of a windy day, with men holding on to their bowler hats, Archer is approached by Rivière. He is the secretary sent to America by the Count to bring the Countess home, but Archer met him during his honeymoon in Europe without realizing his connection to the family. At Archer's office, Rivière explains that he does not really think that Madame Olenska should return to Europe with him, and he asks Archer to use his influence to keep her in America.

At a dinner party, there is talk about the depressed economy destroying Beaufort's business. When Archer hears that Beaufort's failing business will affect Madame Olenska, he flies into a rage at the implication that she is Beaufort's mistress. He has revealed his feelings for her needlessly: she will be affected because she has invested her money with Beaufort.

A message comes that Mrs. Mingott has had a stroke. Archer and May race to see her, only to find out that she is still in fine health. The family is coming to be with her, and when Archer volunteers to meet Countess Olenska's train, May becomes suspicious. In the carriage from the train station, Archer and Olenska kiss. Archer suggests that he wants her with him, but she dismisses his idea, saying that there is no place in the world where they can be together. Archer leaves the carriage before it arrives back at Mrs. Mingott's house.

The Exposure

Sitting in front of the fire with May, Archer reads a book about Japan. He stares at May and thinks about the possibility of her death.

Archer and Countess Olenska meet at a museum. She offers to spend the night with him once before returning to her husband. They agree to meet a few nights later.

The night of the meeting, Archer goes to May while she is at the opera and takes her to a room outside. Just as he is about to confess, she interrupts to tell him that Madame Olenska, having received money from Mrs. Mingott so that she will not have to return to her husband, is leaving for Europe, financially independent. May shows him the letter from Olenska, explaining that she is leaving and cannot be stopped.

Soon, Archer and May give their first society dinner—a farewell dinner for Madame Olenska. Archer assumes that everyone at the dinner knows of his and the Countess's feelings and is there to support his wife in suppressing him. At the end of the evening, Madame Olenska refuses his offer to walk her out to her carriage, choosing to go with her family.

The night of the party, Archer talks to May, expressing his wish to travel on his own. She refuses to let him go by himself, but she does not think she can travel with him because, she reveals, she is pregnant. Although it was confirmed just that day, she told Madame Olenska that she was pregnant two weeks earlier, which explains why she refused to meet with Archer the day they had planned.

The Ensuing Years

The narrator gives a summary of the future of the Archer family: the birth of Theodore and other children and their various career paths, engagements, and marriages. When May dies, Archer, now fifty-seven, honestly mourns her.

His son Theodore phones from Chicago to invite Archer to join him on a trip to Europe. In Paris, Ted tells him that he has arranged to meet with Madame Olenska. Archer is rattled but agrees to go with him. As they walk through the park to go meet the Countess, Ted explains that he knows his father almost threw away his entire life for her but did not; he learned it from May, the day before she died.

Outside Countess Olenska's apartment building, Archer sits on a bench and declines to enter. He looks up at her window and imagines her at the lake, when she did not turn to see him and he did not go to her. Then he stands up and walks away.

CHARACTERS

Newland Archer

Newland Archer is a young lawyer from one of New York's most prominent families. He is played by celebrated British actor Daniel Day-Lewis. He has every had every social advantage and a good education. Outwardly, he seeks to uphold the prevailing social order, but deep inside, he has a subversive streak that encourages him to rebel against society.

At the beginning of the film, the element that keeps Archer socially respectable is his fiancée, May Welland. "May Welland," the narrator explains, "represented for Archer all that was best in their world, all that he honored, and she anchored him to it." He wants their engagement to be announced even before hearing how people gossip about Madame Olenska, though once he realizes he can help her socially he has the announcement made immediately. In general, Archer views May as a well-meaning person who is not bright enough to chafe under the artificial constraints of society.

In Ellen Olenska, Archer sees a reflection of his own self-image. When the social world rejects her for her nonconformity, Madame Olenska stands up for herself. She is willing to divorce her husband to earn her freedom, even if it means a loss of social standing. He starts falling in love with her when she shows her vulnerability, breaking down into tears, empathizing with her as she feels the pressure of social opinion. Though he has never been a social outcast, he can easily imagine himself to be one.

It is when he finds himself falling for Madame Olenska that Archer pushes the most to marry May, to stop himself from committing a social transgression. After they are married, though, he keeps thinking of Olenska, who is now related to him. He makes up reasons to see her alone and plans to run away with her, but May knows him too well by that point. She stops their affair before it begins. Years later, when their son Ted tries to take him to meet Madame Olenska, he says that his mother told him Archer had given up his affair because she had asked him to. Archer mutters, "She never asked," indicating that his fidelity was to the social order, and not to May.

Ted Archer

Theodore Archer, called Ted, is the first son of Newland and May. In Wharton's novel, this character is named Dallas. It is May's pregnancy with him that makes Madame Olenska agree to leave the country and makes Archer give up the idea of pursuing her. As an adult, played by Robert Sean Leonard, Ted convinces his aging father to accompany him on a trip to Europe. In Paris, he casually mentions that he has arranged a meeting with Madame Olenska, knowing from his mother that she is the true love of his father's life. When

Archer balks at meeting her again, Ted is lighthearted. He does not force the issue, but he goes to meet her himself.

Julius Beaufort

Beaufort is played by Stuart Wilson. He is a banker and a romancer of women, in spite of his marriage to Regina Beaufort. Archer becomes jealous of him when he sees Beaufort approaching the house in the country where Madame Olenska is supposed to be living alone. He later flies into a rage when he is told that Madame Olenska will probably need money after Beaufort goes bankrupt, accusing the speaker of implying that she is Beaufort's kept woman. It is clear that Beaufort would like to have Madame Olenska as his mistress, though he is not successful.

Julius Beaufort functions as a dark mirror image of Newland Archer. As Archer finds himself falling for Madame Olenska, he has Beaufort to look to, to remind him of just how ugly it is to be a womanizer.

Regina Beaufort

The wife of Julius Beaufort, she is also a niece of Mrs. Mingott. In the novel, her appeal to Mrs. Mingott to procure a loan for her husband when his business fails is what causes her aunt to have a stroke, though the film presents her stroke as a false alarm.

Sillerton Jackson

Played by Alec McCowen, Jackson is identified early in the film as a man who knows all of the society gossip and lives to spread it around. He gains prestige in this society by spreading malicious stories, surrounding himself with like-minded people who value the naughty thrill of rumor-mongering. Early in the film, Jackson stands out as a the embodiment of society's threat to Ellen Olenska, telling stories about her life in Europe that might or might not be true, but that are not talked about openly.

Larry Lefferts

Lawrence Lefferts, played by Richard E. Grants, is introduced by the narrator as "New York's foremost authority on form," a grand distinction that is put in perspective in the next sentence, which characterizes his opinions about shoe styles. When the Wellands' party to welcome Madame Olenska is ignored by the socially prominent, Archer takes the issue to the van der Luydens, explaining that he is sure Lefferts has pursued a campaign against her just to distract his own wife's suspicious about his behavior. Though Lefferts knows what is and is not socially acceptable, the word of long-established society figures like the van der Luydens can overrule his understanding of what is proper.

Mrs. Manson Mingott

Mrs. Mingott, played by Miriam Margolis, is the widow of Manson Mingott, the mother of May Welland, and the aunt of Regina Beaufort. Wharton's novel gives her first name as "Catherine," though that is never used in the film (she follows the custom of the time of using "Mrs." with her husband's first name). She is the respected matriarch of the family, a woman of such significant social standing that Archer and May feel obliged to immediately bring the news to her when they announce their engagement. Her own social power is not enough, however, to bring people to the party to welcome Madame Olenska to New York once she has been deemed socially toxic.

Madame Olenska lives with Mrs. Mingott for a while in New York. When she leaves the country, it is because Mrs. Mingott, at May's urging, has given her the money she needs to return to Europe.

Ellen Olenska

Madame Olenska, the cousin of May Welland, is played by Michelle Pfeiffer, a casting choice that some critics objected to: the Ellen Olenska of Wharton's novel is dark and mysterious, while Pfeiffer is pale and plays the part with timidity. In the film she is referred to as "Madame Olenska," "Countess Olenska," and "Ellen," depending on who is talking about her, but the narrator of Wharton's novel generally calls her Madame Olenska.

Madame Olenska comes into the film as an unknown quantity. The narrator and the visual design scheme of the film have been used to show that New York society runs by a strict code, but Madame Olenska has been outside that society and therefore is not part of the code. At first, this means that the worst is assumed of her. She is a member of the Welland family, though, and so May, her mother, her grandmother, and her fiancé Newland Archer do what they can to get her accepted, such as talking to social trendsetters like the van der Luydens on her behalf. As she begins to make inroads in New York, she considers formally divorcing the womanizing Polish count to whom she is married, but Archer talks her out of it, fearing what a divorce would do to her reputation, even though it would free her for him to marry.

After Archer's marriage to May, Madame Olenska goes out of her way to avoid Archer, knowing that their mutual attraction can only hurt her cousin and destroy Archer. Eventually, she agrees to accept money from Mrs. Mingott and leave the country, but Archer convinces her to spend one night with him before going. When she hears about May's pregnancy, however, she refuses to break up their marriage, and she leaves without even talking to him. Though her character's motives are kept uncertain throughout the film and Scorsese leaves viewers to wonder if she is willing to steal Archer from her cousin, Madame Olenska turns out to be driven by honor.

Rivière

Archer meets Monsieur Rivière, played by Jonathan Pryce, when he and May are touring Europe after their marriage. Later, Rivière comes to him in New York and explains that he was the secretary who helped Madame Olenska run away from her marriage. He has been sent to America to convince Olenska to return to her husband, but he tells Archer confidentially that he does not think that she should.

Louisa van der Luyden

Mrs. van der Luyden and her husband are among the oldest and most well-established social figures in New York. When Archer tells the couple that Larry Lefferts is unfairly trying to block Madame Olenska from entering society, their sense of justice is offended. They make a point of inviting Olenska to their upcoming party, knowing that people will welcome her if they see that the van der Luydens welcome her.

Henry van der Luyden

Henry van der Luyden is one half of a socially prominent couple that has even more influence than the respected Mrs. Mingott. The Welland family comes to talk to the van der Luydens on the behalf of Madame Olenska, with Newland Archer, who is not married into the family yet, making the case like a lawyer about why the social world is treating

Olenska unfairly. Henry van der Luyden weighs Archer's argument and decides to intercede on Madame Olenska's behalf.

May Welland

Twenty-one-year-old May is Newland Archer's fiancée, played by Winona Ryder. She is part of a socially prominent family, and her grandmother, Mrs. Mingott, is one of the most respected and powerful matrons in town. One of the things that Archer likes about her is that she lacks the imagination to be socially rebellious, and he can therefore count on his upcoming marriage to May to keep him out of trouble. At first, she welcomes his involvement with her cousin, Madame Olenska, encouraging him when he sends her flowers. When he finds himself romantically tempted by her cousin, Archer pressures May to marry him sooner than planned. May, thinking that he is interested in his old flame, identified in the novel as Mrs. Rushworth, offers to release him from their engagement. The film does not hint as strongly as Wharton's book that May might just obtain her mother's approval for the marriage to keep him from straying.

At the beginning of the film, May seems sweet but naïve. She has no aspirations other than to be a dutiful wife. Archer's affair with her cousin brings out a hard and defensive side in her, however. She fights for her marriage without seeming to fight. When Archer tries to tell her about his love for another woman, May interrupts him, and when he tries to make plans to leave the country, to pursue Madame Olenska, she stops him with news of her pregnancy. In each case, it is clear that May knows what he is going to reveal but feels that such a revelation would be bad for their marriage. Even more than cunning, though, she turns out to have been surprisingly dishonest, telling Madame Olenska that she is pregnant weeks before this is confirmed so that she will leave the Archers alone. Years later, she dies from pneumonia contracted while nursing her son Bill. "She died," the narrator says, "thinking the world a good place, full of loving and harmonious households like her own." On her deathbed, she tells her son Ted that she knows that Madame Olenska was the love of Archer's life, something that she never discussed with Archer himself.

Mrs. Welland

Mrs. Welland, played by film veteran Geraldine Chaplin, is May's mother. For the first half of the film, she is an obstacle to the marriage between Newland Archer and her daughter, refusing to give her consent. He considers eloping to get around her restrictions, but May will not do such a thing.

THEMES

Aristocracy

The term *aristocracy* comes from a Greek word, pronounced similarly, meaning rule of the best. Literally, it refers to a government that is controlled by a small privileged class. In common usage, however, it has come to refer to the privileged sector of any society, whether they are political rulers or not.

The Archers, the Wellands, and the other families that populate *The Age of Innocence* certainly embody the concept of American aristocracy. For one thing, they are in control of enormous wealth, and that wealth gives them power. Still, wealth is not enough, in itself, to gain one admission into this social set. As Madame Olenska finds out when she returns from Europe, there are unrecorded codes of behavior that can gain one admission to or exclusion from this group, even if one is born into it, as she was. The film identifies Lawrence Lefferts as having studied the rules of this society, but it also shows how a very powerful person, such as Louisa or Henry van der Luyden, can change these rules if they want.

Conformity

In some cultures, innovation is rewarded. The

Darwinian concept of "survival of the fittest," when applied to society, implies that success depends on showing superior talents. The New York society culture presented in this film, however, is populated with powerful people who can generally do what they want. They have the means to travel the world and acquire whatever interests them. The one thing that keeps the egos of the rich and powerful in check is the social pressure to conform.

The film gives viewers a visual tour of the trappings of wealth, starting with the layers upon layers of the opera house and on through mansions, stables, and gardens. During the Archers' honeymoon, viewers are given a glimpse into the lives of wealthy Europeans, who provide the model for the American upper class, with families that have retained their social position for generations, even centuries. Scorsese examines the lives of the rich with a microscope, knowing, as they know, that they cannot deviate from the standards without losing their social standing.

The film gives two parallel examples of nonconformity in this society. Throughout the film, Scorsese's camera sweeps over portraits and landscapes on the walls of homes that are considered safe to display. Early in the film, at the Beaufort mansion's Crimson Drawing Room, Archer looks over *The Return of Spring*, a painting of some nudes, which the narrator says that Julius Beaufort "had the audacity to hang in plain sight"— he is pushing the edges of conformity, but has not gone far enough to be ostracized. Later, however, when Archer is waiting at Madame Olenska's house for her, he looks over some impressionist artworks that help identify Olenska as being too wild and unconventional for the New York social world.

Obsession

Although Wharton's novel and Scorsese's movie are both interested in the behaviors of a certain class of people at a certain period in American history, they are both held together by the story of Newland Archer's obsession with Ellen Olenska. His interest in her has actually begun before the start of the film. He sees her in her cousin May's box at the opera and immediately feels compelled to go over to where she is, pausing, stunned, when she offers her hand. She mentions their past together. He kissed her once, she tells him, when they were children, though she dismisses the seriousness of this by noting that she was actually in love with his cousin Vandie, "the one who never looked at me."

READ, WATCH, WRITE

- Edith Wharton is referred to by the Web site *A Lit Chick* as the "gossip girl of the Gilded Age." Create a short film about some behavior in your community and add a narrative soundtrack over it, explaining the social significance of the behavior in the way that the narrator of *The Age of Innocence* does.

- Read a young-adult contemporary tale about a romantic triangle, such as Elizabeth Scott's *The Unwritten Rule* or Susan Colasanti's *Something Like Fate*. Make a list of five or more things the characters do in the novel that you think correspond closely to the things the actors do in *The Age of Innocence*. Read excerpts from the novel for your class as you show the relevant scenes from the film to show that behavior is constant although times change.

- Henry James was an American author who wrote about the upper class at the time when Wharton set this novel. Read his book, *The Europeans: A Sketch*, about an American woman like Madame Olenska who returns after living in Europe. Using the James book as a guide, write a scene from the European honeymoon of Archer and May that shows an additional site they might have visited and what they would have done there. Include illustrations that show a possible setting for the scene.

- A formal waltz is used to open the ball at the Beaufort mansion.

Research this style of waltz; teach the moves to ten or more of your classmates and try to reproduce the choreography from the film.

- This film focuses intensely on the subtle emotional problems of its central characters. Make these characters more exciting by writing a short graphic story (that is, in comic book or graphic novel form) about either Newland Archer or Ellen Olenska. At the end of the story, write an explanation to explain why your character is the same person depicted in *The Age of Innocence*.

- Do you think that the time you are living in now will be remembered as an "age of innocence"? Assign students to two different groups to argue the "yes" and "no" positions before the class. Use examples from popular culture or from past cultures to prove your point.

Throughout the film, Archer's obsession with her grows. He arranges times for them to meet for innocent reasons, probably even convincing himself that he has no plans. Each time they meet, though, he is more fascinated by her, even though he knows that they cannot be together without bringing tragic consequences down on both of them. He tries to move his wedding to May forward, to force himself to lose interest in Madame Olenska, but his marriage does little to quench his obsession with her. He ends up lying in order to create occasions for them to be together, and when he goes to the Blenker's farmhouse to see her, he inhales her scent on her parasol and looks enchanted to have this small contact with her, only to find out that it is not hers after all.

In the end, after Archer has broken off any contact with Madame Olenska and has raised his family, he is still unable to face her. The film raises the question of whether he was only obsessed with a pretty woman or truly in love.

Innocence

The "innocence" of the title can be taken two ways. For one thing, Archer and Madame Olenska remain innocent because they both take steps to stop their romance before it goes too far. Even though they plan to spend the night together, the news of May's pregnancy makes each of them reconsider. Madame Olenska accepts her aunt's money and moves away to Europe, and Archer, who had originally planned to follow her, remains innocent by staying by his wife's side.

Wharton also uses "innocence" in the sense of being naïveté. For all of their worldliness, their travels and purchases and parties, the people depicted in this novel are quite childlike in their view of the world. They think that they can know what people are all about through gossip and hearsay, and that love is an inconvenience that can be controlled with enough willpower. Their social position has given them a sense of their own importance that Scorsese and Wharton present as almost quaint.

STYLE

Soundtrack

Scorsese fills the background of this film with a lush soundtrack of orchestral music, matching music popular at the time. The opening scenes set the tone for this, as the characters attend a grand opera that would have been new to them. After Archer leaves the opera, though, the music on the soundtrack continues throughout almost every scene for the rest of the film.

Scorsese eases audiences into this style of music by following the opera scene with a ball at the Beauforts' house, with the orchestral rendition of a waltz by Johann Strauss wafting through every room until Archer reaches the ballroom: there, the music is the background for a formal dance. Similar music continues from then on, though it is not part of the story. The characters are constantly involved with the arts, but they do not attend any more musical events, so the music they hear does not become confused with the music on the soundtrack.

Elmer Bernstein, an award-winning Hollywood composer for hundreds of motion pictures, was nominated for the Academy Award for Best Original Score for *The Age of Innocence*, one of fourteen such nominations over his fifty-year career.

Narration

Narration is often used to fill in plot points that cannot be made clear by presenting the story on screen. In the case of *The Age of Innocence*, the narrator does fill in some plot details for viewers, but more often, she is explaining subtleties about the society the characters inhabit. Wharton's novel is so dense in its explanation of this social setting that it would be virtually impossible to adapt it all to the screen, and the wording used by her narrator was so exact and specific that the filmmakers decided that large pieces of her narration should be included in the film exactly as Wharton wrote it.

Unlike narrators of other films adapted from classic novels, Joanne Woodward does not use a sophisticated or genteel voice. She speaks plainly. This reflects the kind of narrative voice that Wharton used in the book. It is an outsider's voice, looking back with curiosity at the social world of the 1870s from the perspective of the 1920s. Although the narrator knows the rules of the society being shown better than the characters themselves, she has more in common with the viewers than with the characters.

CULTURAL CONTEXT

Films of the 1990s

In the 1990s, the film world, like the world in general, still felt the residual effects of the cultural changes of the late 1960s. That period is remembered as a time when the counterculture ascended to overtake the mainstream culture, a cultural shift that was confirmed when the antiwar movement of the 1960s succeeded and the United States withdrew from the Vietnam war in 1973, soon followed by the resignation of the unpopular President Richard Nixon in 1974. It was an era that made the majority stop and question traditional values. Much good came of this social upheaval, as those who had been kept on the margins of social involvement joined movements to have their rights recognized. The civil rights movement for African Americans, the women's liberation movement, the American Indian movement, and the gay rights movement took form as these social groups, and others, found their voice in the 1960s and 1970s.

Just as social values were being redefined, the 1970s introduced a new generation of filmmakers to the general public: a small group that since then has been dubbed the American new wave. The directors of this generation generally found their start in small independent productions and brought nontraditional values to their projects. Director

Francis Ford Coppola, for example, shot to international fame with a sympathetic look at organized crime in *The Godfather* in 1972. Hal Ashby released a string of movies that questioned social conventions, including *Harold and Maude* in 1971, *The Last Detail* in 1973, *Shampoo* in 1975, and the anti-Vietnam film *Coming Home* in 1978. Brian De Palma spun off his own style of horror film from the works of Alfred Hitchcock with *Carrie* in 1976 and *The Fury* in 1978. Steven Spielberg began the 1970s directing television shows; he moved quickly through one acclaimed television movie and a small independent feature (*Alice Doesn't Live Here Anymore*) before directing one of the biggest box-office blockbusters in history, *Jaws*, in 1975. George Lucas, similarly, went from directing the quirky, character-driven *American Graffiti* in 1973 to the start of one of the most lucrative franchises in film history, *Star Wars*, in 1977. Martin Scorsese showed some indication of his directorial skill with the low-budget exploitation film *Boxcar Bertha* in 1973 and then broke out as a talented artist with *Mean Streets* in 1973.

In the 1980s, the new wave directors became the Hollywood mainstream, as the rebels who had fought to redefine the social order during the previous decades were incorporated into the establishment. During the administration of Ronald Reagan (1981–1989) and on into the presidential administration of Reagan's vice president, George H. W. Bush (1989–1993), films followed society in trying to establish a new relationship with traditional values. They backed away from using the rich as villains, going for a more subtle view of families where wealth was present but not a defining factor, in films such as *Kramer vs. Kramer* in 1979, *Baby Boom* in 1987, and *Hannah and Her Sisters* in 1988. William J. Palmer dubs these films "Yuppie Texts" in his book *The Films of the Eighties*, playing off of the acronym for young urban professionals popular around that time. As the 1980s ended, films like *Wall Street* (1987) and *Bright Lights, Big City* (1988) looked at society's newfound fixation with the dark side of wealth. When *The Age of Innocence* was released in 1993, the rich were social models again in a way they had not been since the counterculture 1960s.

The Postwar Generation of 1920

When Edith Wharton published *The Age of Innocence* in 1920, the world was reeling from the international devastation wrought by the Great War, which is now known as World War I. The war, which ended officially in November 1918, was referred to by British politician David Lloyd George when it was over with the hope that future generations would look back on it as "the war to end all wars." It is easy to see why people around the world might have taken George's phrase to heart, as World War I represented a level of military conflict that had never been seen before. The scope of the war was immense, involving more than 100 countries across five continents. In all, eight and a half million men were killed and another twenty-one million were wounded. These grand statistics, however, do not indicate the psychological effect of the first war of the modern era. Advanced techniques in warfare ranged from the airplane, which could drop tons of explosives onto targets virtually anywhere, to the use of chemical weapons, such as mustard gas, which caused bleeding in the lungs and led to near-instant drowning.

Veterans returned from the war having seen horrors that they could never have imagined. In literature, a generation of writers that came to be called the Lost Generation reflected the disillusionment that was felt all over the world as a result of World War I. Those writers, including Ernest Hemingway, F. Scott Fitzgerald, John Dos Passos, and T. S. Eliot, tried to reflect the sense of despair that had overcome an entire generation of intellectuals. At the time that the Lost Generation was starting to publish works about the hopelessness of their time, Wharton was looking back fifty years, to a time when the children of affluence felt that social pressure was the worst thing they faced, calling it the age of innocence.

CRITICAL OVERVIEW

Critics generally approached this film with mixed feelings. It is considered a surprising, ambitious achievement for director Martin Scorsese, but most found it to fall short of its mark. Most critical responses fall between Jonathan Rosenbaum of the *Chicago Reader*, who praises it as an "ambitious and sumptuous" film but ultimately declares it "a noble failure," and Vincent Canby of the *New York Times*, who declares, "*The Age of Innocence* isn't perfect, but it's a robust gamble that pays off."

Many of the critics who were impressed with this film expressed admiration for the way it avoided the coldness of other adaptations of literary classics, especially those produced by Ismail Merchant and James Ivory, starting with their adaptation of Henry James's *The Europeans* in 1979. "As you'd expect from Scorsese, it's no waxworks wannabe classic," Michael Wilmington states in the *Chicago Tribune*. "It has a pulse, a volatile current." Desson Howe of the *Washington Post* notes the treatments of the past given in film by "the stuffy Merchant-Ivory team" before declaring, "What a sublime pleasure it is … to experience *The Age of Innocence* through the eyes of Martin Scorsese." He explains his pleasure in it: "Instead of *Masterpiece Theatre*—style fawning, he fills this movie with visual flow, masterful cinematography and assured direction. There's an alert, thinking presence behind the camera."

Still, there were critics who found that Scorsese's good intentions could not overcome the flaws in his approach. In the *Nation*, Stuart Klawans writes that Scorsese treats his rich socialites too respectfully, as if they really are the superior beings that they seem to think they are. "He's deferential," Klawans says, "as if those stiffs from Fifth Avenue were somehow better than a boy from Elizabeth Street"—a reference to the tough hustlers of Scorsese's first film, *Mean Streets*. "The style becomes as repressed as the characters themselves and is then capped by a further repression of the lead actors." After airing his complaints, though, Klawans admits, "None of this means that *The Age of Innocence* is a failure. In a sense, Scorsese has reached the stage at which there can be no complete failures, since everything he makes has relevance to his career."

Owen Gleiberman, in *Entertainment Weekly*, gives the film an overall grade of *B+*, claiming that, for all its artistry, "*The Age of Innocence* isn't entirely successful." He feels that there are too many meetings between Archer and Madame Olenska after their original breakup, giving the last half of the film a fragmented feeling. "Scorsese and coscreenwriter Jay Cocks would have been wise to drop a few of the later incidents and linger more over the dramatic texture," Gleiberman explains, "As it is, the second half of *The Age of Innocence* comes at us in so many bits and pieces that it fails to achieve the overwhelming sense of loss that is the story's driving emotion."

Despite almost universal approval for Martin Scorsese's daring in taking on a project so far out of his customary field, and for his artistic achievements for the material, he was not even nominated for a best director Academy Award, nor was the picture nominated for best picture. However, *Time* magazine declared it the best picture of 1993, beating out *Schindler's List*, which won the best picture award from the Academy that year. The only Academy Award won by the picture was for best costume design. The two leads, Daniel Day-Lewis and Michelle Pfeiffer, were not even nominated, though Winona Ryder was nominated for best supporting actress. At the Golden Globes, Scorsese and Pfeiffer were nominated, and Ryder won. Scorsese and Pfeiffer did receive the Elvira Notari Prize at the Venice Film Festival.

SOURCES

Canby, Vincent, "The Age of Innocence: Grand Passions and Good Manners," in *New York Times*, September 17, 1993, p. 1.

Ebert, Roger, *Scorsese by Ebert*, University of Chicago Press, 2008, p. 287.

Gleiberman, Owen, "The Age of Innocence," in *Entertainment Weekly*, September 17, 1993, http://www.ew.com/ew/article/0,,308064,00.html (accessed October 11, 2010).

Howe, Desson, "The Age of Innocence," in *Washington Post*, September 17, 1993, http://www.washingtonpost.com/wp-srv/style/longterm/movies/videos/theageofinnocence (accessed October 11, 2010).

Klawans, Stuart, "The Age of Innocence," in *Nation*, Vol. 257, No. 10, October 4, 1993, pp. 364–66.

Palmer, William J., "The Yuppie Texts," in *The Films of the Eighties*, Southern Illinois University Press, 1993, pp. 280–307.

Rosenbaum, Jonathan, "The Age of Innocence," in *Chicago Reader*, http://www.chicagoreader.com/chicago/the-age-ofinnocence/Film?oid=1054994 (accessed October 11, 2010).

Scorsese, Martin, and Jay Cocks, *The Age of*

Innocence, Columbia Pictures, 1993.

Wilmington, Michael, "*The Age of Innocence*: Martin Scorsese's Lush Romance Seethes With Suppressed Passion," in *Chicago Tribune*, September 17, 1983.

"World War I Casualty and Death Tables," in *The Great War and the Shaping of the Twentieth Century*, Public Broadcasting System, http://www.pbs.org/greatwar/resources/casdeath_po] (accessed October 24, 2010).

FURTHER READING

Lee, A. Robert, "Watching Manners: Martin Scorsese's *The Age of Innocence*, and Edith Wharton's *The Age of Innocence*," in *The Classic Novel from Page to Screen*, edited by Robert Giddings and Erica Sheen, Manchester University Press, 2000, pp. 163–88.

> Lee's study focuses on the changes Scorsese made to the source material for *The Age of Innocence*, finding his adaptation to be an excellent one.

Scorsese, Martin, "*The Age of Innocence*—A Personal Journey," in *Scorsese on Scorsese*, edited by Ian Christie and David Thompson, Faber and Faber, 2003, pp. 176–97.

> Scorsese tells of his involvement in the making of this film, from the time it was proposed by writer Jay Cocks in 1980 through the scripting, casting, and shooting processes.

Scorsese, Martin, and Jay Cocks, *"The Age of Innocence": A Portrait of the Film Based on the Novel by Edith Wharton*, edited by Robin Standefer, Newmarket Press, 1993.

> The shooting script of the film is available in paperback form by itself, but this deluxe edition, with production photographs by Philip J.

Caruso, includes the script plus many photographs from the 1800s that inspired specific set and costume designs.

Updike, John, "Archer's Way," in *Edith Wharton's The Age of Innocence*, edited by Harold Bloom, Chelsea House Publishers, 2005, pp. 133–40.

Although it does not mention the film version, this study, by one of America's greatest writers, is rich with background information about Wharton and the process of producing the novel.

SUGGESTED SEARCH TERMS

Edith Wharton

Wharton AND Martin Scorsese

Scorsese AND Michelle Pfeiffer

Scorsese AND Jay Cocks

The Age of Innocence AND Daniel Day-Lewis

Edith Wharton AND film

Age of Innocence AND Michael Ballhaus

Scorsese AND Gilded Age

New York AND 1870s

Edith Wharton AND manners